THOMAS CRANE PUBLIC LIBRARY
QUINCY MASS
CITY APPROPRIATION

Environment in Focus

Food Supplies

Cheryl Jakab

Marshall Cavendish
Benchmark
New York

This edition first published in 2011 in the United States of America by
Marshall Cavendish Benchmark
An imprint of Marshall Cavendish Corporation

All rights reserved.

No part of this publication may be reproduced, stored in a retrieval system or transmitted, in any form or by any means, electronic, mechanical, photocopying, recording, or otherwise, without the prior permission of the copyright owner. Request for permission should be addressed to the Publisher, Marshall Cavendish Corporation, 99 White Plains Road, Tarrytown, NY 10591.
Tel: (914) 332-8888, fax: (914) 332-1888.

Website: www.marshallcavendish.us

This publication represents the opinions and views of the author based on Cheryl Jakab's personal experience, knowledge, and research. The information in this book serves as a general guide only. The author and publisher have used their best efforts in preparing this book and disclaim liability rising directly and indirectly from the use and application of this book.

Other Marshall Cavendish Offices:
Marshall Cavendish International (Asia) Private Limited, 1 New Industrial Road, Singapore 536196 • Marshall Cavendish International (Thailand) Co Ltd. 253 Asoke, 12th Flr, Sukhumvit 21 Road, Klongtoey Nua, Wattana, Bangkok 10110, Thailand • Marshall Cavendish (Malaysia) Sdn Bhd, Times Subang, Lot 46, Subang Hi-Tech Industrial Park, Batu Tiga, 40000 Shah Alam, Selangor Darul Ehsan, Malaysia

Marshall Cavendish is a trademark of Times Publishing Limited

All websites were available and accurate when this book was sent to press.

Library of Congress Cataloging-in-Publication Data

Jakab, Cheryl.
  Food supplies / Cheryl Jakab.
    p. cm. — (Environment in focus)
  Includes index.
  Summary: "Discusses the environmental issue of food supplies and how to create a sustainable way of living"—Provided by publisher.
  ISBN 978-1-60870-090-5
  1. Food-supply—Environmental aspects—Juvenile literature. 2. Produce trade—Environmental aspects—Juvenile literature. 3. Sustainable agriculture—Juvenile literature. I. Title.
  HD9000.5.J34 2011
  338.1'9—dc22
                                    2009042298

First published in 2010 by
MACMILLAN EDUCATION AUSTRALIA PTY LTD
15–19 Claremont Street, South Yarra 3141

Visit our website at www.macmillan.com.au or go directly to www.macmillanlibrary.com.au

Associated companies and representatives throughout the world.

Copyright © Cheryl Jakab 2010

Edited by Margaret Maher
Text and cover design by Cristina Neri, Canary Graphic Design
Page layout by Domenic Lauricella
Photo research by Sarah Johnson
Illustrations by Domenic Lauricella
Maps courtesy of Geo Atlas

Printed in the United States

Acknowledgments
The author and the publisher are grateful to the following for permission to reproduce copyright material:

Front cover photograph: Combine Plowing soybean field, Colorado, Glowimages/Getty Images

© Gene Blevins/CORBIS, 19; © Natalie Fobes/CORBIS, 18; © Wolfgang Kaehler/CORBIS, 7 (top), 13; © Karen Kasmauski/CORBIS, 20; © Kevin Steele/Aurora Photos/CORBIS, 27; © Dung Vo Trung/Sygma/CORBIS, 7 (bottom), 21; Dorling Kindersley/Getty Images, 6 (top), 25; Brian Skerry/National Geographic/Getty Images, 16; Maxfocus/iStockphoto, 8; © qldian/iStockphoto, 6 (bottom), 17; © Jupiter Images, 11, 26;© Aaron McCoy/Jupiter Images, 22; © Peter Charlesworth/OnAsia /Jupiter Images, 7 (middle), 9; © Roulland/Jupiter Images, 10; Lonely Planet Images/Tom Cockrem, 15; REUTERS/Enrique Castro-Mendivil, 5; REUTERS/Erik de Castro, 24; REUTERS/Bob Strong, 23; © Monkey Business Images/Shutterstock, 28; © Jiri Vaclavek/Shutterstock, 29; Photo by Lynn Betts, USDA Natural Resources Conservation Service, 12, 14.

While every care has been taken to trace and acknowledge copyright, the publisher tenders their apologies for any accidental infringement where copyright has proved untraceable. Where the attempt has been unsuccessful, the publisher welcomes information that would redress the situation.

Please note
At the time of printing, the Internet addresses appearing in this book were correct. Owing to the dynamic nature of the Internet, however, we cannot guarantee that all these addresses will remain correct.

1 3 5 6 4 2

Contents

Environment in Focus	4
What's the Issue? Increasing Demand for Food	5
Food Supply Issues Around the Globe	6

ISSUE 1
Environmental Costs of Food — 8

ISSUE 2
Decreasing Land for Crops — 12

ISSUE 3
Impacts of Overfishing — 16

ISSUE 4
Climate Change and Food — 20

ISSUE 5
Food Miles — 24

What Can You Do? Think Global, Eat Local	28
Toward a Sustainable Future	30
Websites	30
Glossary	31
Index	32

Glossary Words
When a word is printed in **bold**, you can look up its meaning in the Glossary on page 31.

Environment in Focus

Hi there! This is Earth speaking. Will you spare a moment to listen to me? I have some very important things to discuss.

We must focus on some urgent environmental problems! All living things depend on my environment, but the way you humans are living at the moment, I will not be able to keep looking after you.

The issues I am worried about are:
- large ecological footprints
- damage to natural wonders
- widespread pollution in the environment
- the release of **greenhouse gases** into the **atmosphere**
- poor management of waste
- environmental damage caused by food production

My challenge to you is to find a **sustainable** way of living. Read on to find out what people around the world are doing to try to help.

Fast Fact
Concerned people in local, national, and international groups are trying to understand how our way of life causes environmental problems. This important work helps us learn how to live more sustainably now and in the future.

What's the Issue? Increasing Demand for Food

The world demand for food is increasing as the human population increases. However, the amount of food produced in many areas is decreasing due to environmental damage.

Increasing Population and Food Production

The human population increased from about 1.5 billion to more than 6 billion people between 1900 and 2000. During this time, food production also increased to keep up with the demand of the growing population.

The increase in food production has had a huge impact on Earth's environments. Many areas that produced good crops in the past are now **degraded**. **Overfishing** has damaged important fisheries. Water and oil shortages and **climate change** are further impacting food production.

Fast Fact
In 2009, it was estimated that nearly one billion people in the world were undernourished.

Food Shortages

Today, food shortages are becoming widespread in many regions of the world. Many people live without a secure supply of food.

In some countries, food shortages have caused major protests.

Food Supply Issues

The most urgent food supply issues around the globe include:
- the damage done to the environment by food production
- decreasing **soil fertility** and increasing **erosion**
- decreasing numbers of fish and other sea life due to overfishing
- the effect that climate change has on food supply
- the impacts of transporting food

ISSUE 5
Britain
Food is being transported over increasing distances, adding to greenhouse gas emissions. See pages 24–27.

Fast Fact
About one-third of the ice-free land on Earth is used to produce food for people. Of this land, about one-third is used for grazing animals.

ISSUE 3
Mediterranean Sea
Uncontrolled fishing is endangering sharks. See pages 16–19.

Around the Globe

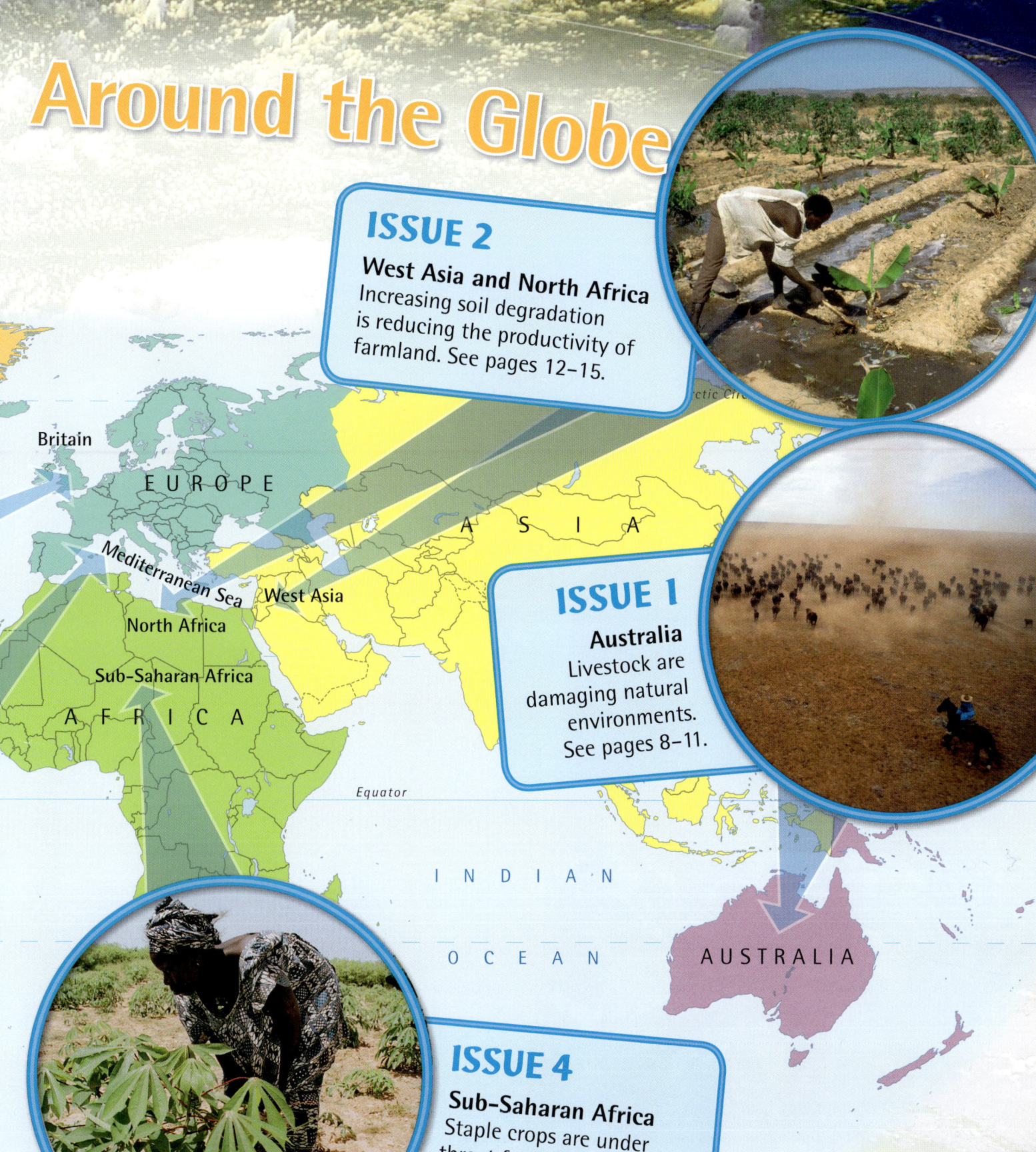

ISSUE 2

West Asia and North Africa
Increasing soil degradation is reducing the productivity of farmland. See pages 12–15.

ISSUE 1

Australia
Livestock are damaging natural environments. See pages 8–11.

ISSUE 4

Sub-Saharan Africa
Staple crops are under threat from climate change. See pages 20–23.

ISSUE 1

Environmental Costs of Food

Producing the amount of food needed by the world's population has begun to damage the environment.

Taking Over More Land

About one-third of the ice-free land on Earth is now used to produce food for people. This means that very little natural environment is left for other living things, and that area continues to decrease. The limited available land restricts the amount of food that can be produced.

Animals in Feedlots

Increasingly, animals that are used to produce food are kept in **feedlots**. Animals in feedlots are fed grains and vegetable crops. This has a greater impact on the environment than grazing. It also affects food production. A single cow can eat about 22 pounds (10 kilograms) of corn each day. This uses up corn that could be eaten by humans.

Animals raised in feedlots are less healthy than animals that graze on pastures.

Fast Fact
In 2006, livestock provided about one-third of the world's protein foods and used about one-third of the world's productive land.

The hard hooves of grazing animals, such as cattle, can cause soil erosion.

CASE STUDY

Grazing and the Australian Environment

Meat from grazing animals, such as cattle and sheep, is a good source of food. However, producing it can be very hard on the environment.

Damage to the Environment

The Australian environment is easily damaged by sheep and cattle. Native Australian grasses are damaged by the animals' hard hooves. Sheep also eat the grasses down to a much lower point than native animals. This kills the plants and adds to soil erosion because the plant roots no longer hold the soil in place.

Early Grazing and Overgrazing

Early grazing and overgrazing are also causing problems. Early grazing occurs when animals are grazed on grasses that are very young and easily damaged. Overgrazing occurs when too many animals are grazed on an area of land.

ISSUE 1

Fast Fact
Rabbits were introduced to Australia from Europe in 1858. They have damaged **rangelands** by digging burrows and eating plants that help prevent soil erosion.

ISSUE 1

Toward a Sustainable Future: Protecting Farmland and Wilderness

The extent of human activity needs to be controlled in order to keep some areas of land as protected wilderness.

Improved Farming Practices

New approaches are being developed to improve farming practices. For example, some farmers are now paid to protect soils and watercourses on their lands. Planting trees achieves all of these aims in many areas.

Sustainable Meat Production

Meat production needs to be more sustainable to reduce the impacts on the environment. The world's rangelands are already grazed at or beyond their limits. One way to ensure sustainable meat production is to reduce the amount of meat we eat. This would reduce the numbers of grazing animals required.

Fast Fact
Mixed farms support a variety of crops and animals. Animals such as goats, sheep, and cows can form part of a sustainable system. These animals eat weeds and supply droppings as a natural **fertilizer** for crops.

A pasture that is grazed within its limits can remain healthy and productive.

Fast Fact
Eating a diet of mostly vegetables and fruits can help prevent obesity, heart disease, cancer, and many other health problems. It is also better for the environment.

Choosing to eat more vegetables and less meat is better for the environment and for you.

CASE STUDY
Plant-Based Diets

Plant-based diets consist mostly of plant food with little or no meat. If everyone ate plant-based diets, much less land would be needed for grazing animals.

Food and Wilderness

As the human population grows, both adequate food and intact wilderness are needed. Changing food production from animal foods to plant-based foods has many advantages. For example, it reduces the impacts on rangeland environments. Plant-based diets can also be healthier than those based on large servings of meat.

Changing Habits

Getting people to change their eating habits is not easy. However, education can help people make informed choices. People need to understand how eating meat threatens **food security** and wilderness areas. People who eat meat can make choices that are better for the environment. This includes limiting the amount of meat they eat and not eating meat from animals raised in feedlots.

ISSUE 1

ISSUE 2

Decreasing Land for Crops

Around the world, the amount of land available for growing crops is decreasing. Many food-growing areas that were productive in the past are now degraded or unusable. This is creating a food supply crisis.

Soil Degradation

Soil degradation is one of the major reasons for the food supply crisis. Increased use of machinery, artificial fertilizers, and irrigation has increased the amount of food produced in many areas. However, in many places these farming techniques have damaged soils in the process.

Limits to Land

The amount of land available for agriculture has reached its limits. More than half of the cropland in the United States is now used to produce animal feed. An increasing amount is being used to grow **biofuel crops**. This further reduces food crop production.

Fast Fact
China's grain production decreased by 44 million tons between 1998 and 2004. In 2004 China imported 8 million tons of grains. In 2008 this increased to nearly 10 million tons.

Farmland with severely damaged soil cannot be used to grow crops.

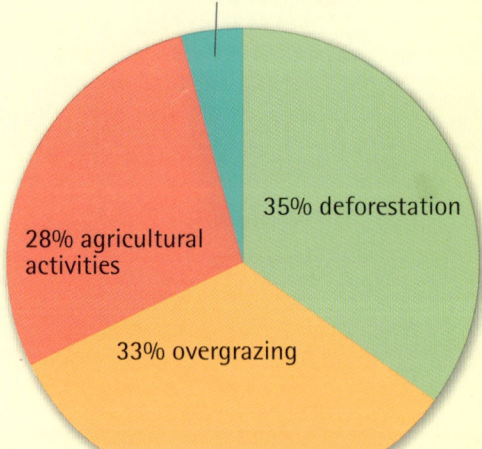

The Main Causes of Soil Degradation

- 4% industrialization
- 35% deforestation
- 33% overgrazing
- 28% agricultural activities

The main causes of soil degradation are deforestation and overgrazing.

Irrigation is needed to provide water for crops in many parts of West Asia and North Africa.

CASE STUDY
Damage Due to Irrigation

The region of West Asia and North Africa is the single largest dryland area in the world. In dryland areas, rainfall is low. There are few permanent rivers. Much of the West Asia and North Africa region has shallow and infertile soil.

By the 1990s, about 35 percent of the cropland in the region was **intensively cropped** using irrigation. This has severely degraded the poor soil.

Effects of Irrigation

Large-scale irrigation has increased crop production in many areas. However, irrigation and poorly managed drainage also cause problems, such as declining water quality, depleted **aquifers**, and increasing **salinity**. Intensive cropping has taken nutrients from the soil, leading to soil degradation. Loss of soil fertility is now widespread.

ISSUE 2

Fast Fact
The region of West Asia and North Africa cannot produce enough food for its population. It must import food for its people to survive.

ISSUE 2

Toward a Sustainable Future: Restoring the Land

Restoring the land requires better-managed farming to improve the soil.

Improving Soil

Lightly degraded soil can be improved by using **crop rotation**. Farmers can also reduce practices that disturb the soil, such as plowing. Moderately damaged land requires complete changes in farming practices. For example:

- Planting crops early means soil is left bare for less time. This helps prevent erosion.
- Planting crops across slopes decreases erosion caused by water runoff.
- Planting hedges or trees decreases erosion by sheltering the soil from winds.

Organic Matter in Soil

One of the main components of fertile soil is **organic matter**. Organic matter can be put back into overworked soils by:

- leaving straw or other plant material on the ground after harvest
- including grasses and **cover crops** in crop rotations
- applying animal manure, **compost**, or **sewage** sludge

Cover crops like this one in the United States can add organic matter to soil and help prevent erosion.

Fast Fact
Using crop rotation can increase the amount of food produced on farms. This is because different plants add and remove different nutrients from soils.

Velvet beans are good to eat and planting them improves soil.

CASE STUDY
Velvet Bean Cover Crops in Benin

The velvet bean is one of the most popular cover crops used today. Thousands of farmers in Benin, West Africa, use velvet bean crops to control weeds and improve soil fertility.

Bean crops increase fertility by adding nutrients to the soil. These nutrients can be used by other crops, such as maize, as they grow. This results in higher crop yield so farmers have more to sell after each harvest.

Cover Crops

Cover crops are grown after food or commercial crops have been harvested. They hold the soil together and add nutrients. Velvet beans are a good cover crop because they require little extra labor. They also help control weeds by pushing out the weed plants.

Fast Fact
Velvet bean seeds were first made available to farmers in Benin by the aid agency Sasakawa Africa Association.

ISSUE 3

Impacts of Overfishing

Overfishing has had severe impacts on rivers and ocean systems across the globe.

Increasing Fish Harvests

Fish harvests in 1950 were about 19.6 million tons (20 million tonnes) worldwide. By 1989 that figure had increased to about 88 million tons (90 million t). Since the 1990s fish harvests have slowed, barely keeping up with our population growth.

Current fishing levels and techniques are putting a strain on all marine **ecosystems**. This includes deep-sea fishing that dredges the ocean floor, damaging the ocean habitat.

Bycatch

When commercial fishers catch animals that are not their desired catch, they call those animals bycatch. These unwanted animals are thrown back into the water dead, dying, or injured. Using huge drifting nets to capture ocean fish has been made illegal because these nets collect large numbers of bycatch.

Many sharks are killed when they are caught as bycatch in fishing nets.

Fast Fact
Tens of millions of sharks are killed for their fins every year. Many shark fishers cut the fins off the shark and then throw the shark overboard to die.

More than 40 percent of sharks, including hammerhead sharks, in the Mediterranean are threatened by uncontrolled fishing.

CASE STUDY
Sharks in Danger

Today, many sharks are in danger in the Mediterranean Sea. This is due to uncontrolled fishing. Even critically endangered shark **species** can be caught in Mediterranean waters without controls.

Targeted Catch and Bycatch

Sharks are now deliberately targeted and caught for food as well as being caught accidentally as bycatch. This has led to overfishing of sharks. Sharks are particularly vulnerable to overfishing because they grow and reproduce slowly.

Effects on the Ecosystem

The disappearance of sharks can have negative effects on the whole marine ecosystem. Sharks eat many species of fish. Removing sharks disrupts the **food web** by allowing the numbers of these fish to rise. This can lead to the disappearance of some species and increased numbers of others as the balance of the ecosystem changes.

Fast Fact
The populations of some species of sharks in the North Atlantic Ocean have decreased by as much as 99 percent in the past thirty years.

ISSUE 3

ISSUE 3

Toward a Sustainable Future: Sustainable Fishing

Sustainable fishing methods help prevent overfishing. These methods include fish farming and targeted fishing, which does not trap unwanted species as bycatch.

Fish Farming

Fish farms raise fish commercially, so that the natural populations are not depleted. Fish farming is a sustainable fishing method. However, it must be managed carefully, since it can lead to disease if done in the ocean. It is better to keep farmed fish away from wild fish.

Reducing Bycatch

Harvesting seafood and fish in ways that reduce bycatch is less harmful to other sea creatures. Fishing techniques that reduce bycatch include using pots and traps, hook-and-line fishing, and diving. Fishers can also use nets that are designed to target specific schools of fish.

Fish farming is a sustainable fishing method that now supplies us with almost half the fish we eat.

Fast Fact

Deep-sea sharks are targeted for a substance in their livers called squalene, or shark liver oil. This substance is used as an ingredient in cosmetics, including lip gloss.

The *Oceana Ranger* is one of the ships Oceana uses to visit and document marine environments.

CASE STUDY

Campaigning for Fisheries and Oceans

Today, many activists are campaigning to restore fisheries and protect ecosystems in the world's oceans.

Fishery Observers

Many activists are calling for fishery observer programs. This involves independent scientists traveling on fishing boats to record what is caught and discarded. This would help researchers calculate the numbers of different species that are taken.

Better Management of Fisheries

The international conservation group Oceana is campaigning for better management of oceans and shark fisheries. They are encouraging governments to address shark bycatch problems and reduce demand for shark products. International cooperation is needed when animals travel over large areas of the ocean, as sharks and whales do. These animals move through oceans belonging to many countries, so their protection needs to be based on international agreements.

Fast Fact
Many people across the world think whale harvesting should be completely banned. They see it as unnecessary and cruel.

ISSUE 3

Climate Change and Food

ISSUE 4

Climate change is predicted to decrease food crop and animal product yields worldwide.

Droughts and Climate Change

Many droughts are devastating crops across Africa, Central America, Australia, and Southeast Asia. Scientists believe these droughts are caused by new climate patterns. In South Asia climate change is expected to reduce almost every major crop by 5 to 10 percent.

Less Grain for Export

The reduced crops mean that China and India are now exporting less grain. These countries need to make sure their own people have enough to eat. China is also importing grain. The United States and Europe also have smaller stockpiles of grain now than in the recent past. This adds to the problem of reduced crops.

Fast Fact
More than 3 billion people live on two dollars a day or less. They spend up to 70 percent of their income on food. This means that small rises in food prices can quickly become life-threatening.

Drought has contributed to food shortages in Africa, where it is becoming harder to grow crops.

Production of cassava is under threat across Africa from brown streak virus.

CASE STUDY

Cassava Crops in Sub-Saharan Africa

Cassava is the main **food staple** for many of Africa's poorest people. However, a disease of cassava plants in Tanzania is now spreading to other parts of sub-Saharan Africa.

Providing Food During Climate Change

Cassava is a root vegetable that can grow in poor soil. It also survives droughts better than most crops. This means it can provide food in times of climate change. However, cassava crops are now being damaged by the brown streak virus.

Cassava Brown Streak Virus

The cassava brown streak virus is a disaster for Africa. The disease does not show on the plant as the crop grows. It is only when the farmers begin to harvest that they find there is no crop under the ground. Between 2002 and 2007, cassava production was reduced by up to 80 percent.

ISSUE 4

Fast Fact
More than 5 million children a year die of hunger. That is about one child every five seconds.

ISSUE 4

Toward a Sustainable Future: Adapting Food Production to Climate Change

Strategies for adapting food production to climate change will vary across the world. They will depend on people's needs, cultures, population, and climates. Strategies being developed include:

- growing a wider range of food crops rather than relying on one crop that might fail
- storing seed in case of disasters
- developing crops that resist damage from insects and developing rice plants that grow on dry land rather than in water
- increasing the eating of insects as an alternative to other animal products
- encouraging heirloom seed-saving networks that preserve less common varieties of seeds

Sustainable Food and Agriculture Project

The organization Friends of the Earth is running the Sustainable Food and Agriculture Project. The project includes preserving small mixed farms that provide food for their local area. This can reduce reliance on imported goods.

Fast Fact
By 2030, southern Africa could lose more than 30 percent of its main food crop, maize, due to climate change.

Small-scale mixed farms can add to local food supplies.

Fast Fact
A disease called potato blight killed about half the potato crop in Ireland in the 1840s. It caused up to one million deaths in the Great Potato Famine.

The cold temperatures in Norway will help preserve the seeds in the Global Seed Vault by keeping them frozen.

CASE STUDY
Norway's Seed Store

On the Norwegian island of Spitsbergen a seed store has been created to prevent the extinction of plant species that are grown for food.

Global Seed Vault
The Global Seed Vault will store seeds of up to 3 million crop varieties. In case of a global catastrophe, such as climate change, these seeds would enable humans to regrow crops. They also help to maintain crop diversity.

Crop Diversity
Crop diversity lessens the impact of plant diseases. Most large farms today plant only one type of crop, such as wheat, rice, or corn. If some plants become diseased, the infection can easily spread to the whole crop. However, other varieties of the crop may not be affected by the same disease. Saving seed from different varieties helps prevent the extinction of food crops.

ISSUE 5

Food Miles

The idea of food miles was developed to highlight the impact of food transportation on the environment. Exhaust from vehicles is adding to greenhouse gas emissions.

Energy for Food Transportation

Food miles describe the energy required for food transportation. Food that has been transported long distances can look the same as a local product. However, it can have very different impacts on the environment. For example, trucks used to transport food burn fossil fuels, resulting in increased greenhouse gas emissions.

Food in Developed Countries

Most people in **developed countries** have access to almost every food product they can imagine. Much of this food is transported great distances. High prices are paid for out-of-season foods, such as cherries in the winter. However, out-of-season foods must be transported from other parts of the world. This adds many food miles.

Fast Fact
The average American meal travels about 1,500 food miles to get from "farm to plate."

The total environmental impact of food includes the energy required for transportation.

Many foods, such as fruits, are transported long distances to reach shops in Britain.

CASE STUDY
Transporting Food

In Britain, the amount of food transported by road has increased by 23 percent in the past twenty years. On average, the distance the food is transported has increased by 65 percent.

Changes in Food Supply

The increase in transport is linked to changes in Britain's food supply. The main change has been an increase in international trade. This allows big supermarkets to provide out-of-season and exotic foods all year round. However, these foods are transported over long distances.

British farmers today could produce 62 percent of the country's food. However, much of the food they produce is exported. This means even more food is imported. Eighty percent of the food sold in London is imported from overseas, including apples from New Zealand and meat from Brazil.

Fast Fact
Today, each British person makes about 221 trips to the grocery store each year. These trips have an average length of 4 miles (6.4 km). They also add to food miles.

ISSUE 5

Toward a Sustainable Future: Increasing Local Production

Increasing the amount of food grown locally can reduce food miles. It can also help improve food security in cities and towns.

Urban Agriculture

Urban agriculture involves growing food in cities and towns. This reduces food miles and lessens people's reliance on distant sources for food. About 15 percent of the world's food is now grown in urban areas.

Farming in the city also brings other benefits. These could include making use of the abundant supply of fertilizer in the form of sewage.

Farmers' Markets

Locally run farmers' markets are providing local food for more and more people across the world. An estimated one billion people in cities worldwide now grow plants to eat or to sell locally.

Urban farming reduces the need for food transportation and helps make cities more pleasant places.

Fast Fact
Tim Lang, who developed the idea of food miles, is campaigning for food miles to be shown on all supermarket products. This would let people see how much energy was used to transport the food they buy.

A farmers' market can be a good place to buy foods grown within 100 miles of your home.

CASE STUDY
The 100-Mile Diet

Alisa Smith and James MacKinnon live in Vancouver, Canada. In 2005 they began buying all their food and drink from places within 100 miles (160 km) of their home. They wanted to eat a diet that was more environmentally friendly than the average North American diet. Ingredients in a typical North American meal are transported an average of 1,490 miles (2,400 km).

Most of the food Smith and MacKinnon ate was grown without artificial fertilizer or pesticides. They prepared all their food themselves. They also preserved fresh food for winter so that they rarely had to buy groceries.

Interest in the 100-Mile Diet

Many people have started their own versions of the 100-mile diet. Usually people find they eat a wider variety of foods and also eat more fresh foods, particularly vegetables.

Fast Fact
The ingredients for a typical British meal traveled less than one-sixtieth of the food miles when sourced locally.

ISSUE 5

What Can You Do?
Think Global, Eat Local

Fast Fact
In 2008, Natural England supported the Year of Food and Farming in Education in the United Kingdom. This program aimed to give school children contact with farms and promote healthy living.

Buying and eating locally produced food helps local producers as well as the planet. You can make a difference. Whenever possible, look for food that is:
- locally grown
- fresh and in season

Buy Environmentally Friendly Products

Check food labels to see if the sources are environmentally friendly. For example, you can look for products that are certified as organic. This means the food has been grown without artificial fertilizer or pesticides.

You can also:
- check with your fish supplier to make sure the fish comes from a sustainable source
- reduce meat consumption by eating smaller portions and eating it less often
- choose products with the minimum packaging

The information on food packaging can help you figure out how far the food has been transported.

In-season local produce can be preserved and stored for later use.

Learn What Is In Season

When you eat locally grown food, you eat food that is in season. Fresh fruit has more flavor than fruit that has been refrigerated and transported from far away. Locally produced winter foods, such as pumpkin or cauliflower soup, are good for your health and for the environment.

Make use of foods you can grow in the different seasons in your area. You could make a chart of foods that people you know grow for themselves. This can include fruits and nuts grown on trees as well as herbs and vegetables grown in gardens.

Preserve Extra

When seasonal fruits and vegetables are harvested there is often more than you can eat. The surplus can be preserved for storage. If you do not have a garden of your own, local markets are a good source of seasonal produce.

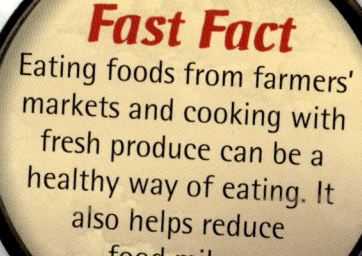

Fast Fact
Eating foods from farmers' markets and cooking with fresh produce can be a healthy way of eating. It also helps reduce food miles.

Toward a Sustainable Future

Well, I hope you now see that if you take up my challenge your world will be a better place. There are many ways to work toward a sustainable future. Imagine a world with:
- a sustainable ecological footprint
- places of natural heritage protected for the future
- no more environmental pollution
- less greenhouse gas in the air, reducing global warming
- zero waste and efficient use of resources
- a secure food supply for all

This is what you can achieve if you work together with my natural systems.

We must work together to live sustainably. That will mean a better environment and a better life for all living things on Earth, now and in the future.

Websites

For further information on food supplies, visit the following websites.
- Sustainable Food http://food.change.org
- Friends of the Earth www.foe.org.au/sustainable-food/
- Sustainable Food Laboratory www.sustainablefoodlab.org
- Oceana http://na.oceana.org/en

Glossary

aquifers
Natural underground chambers that contain water.

atmosphere
The layers of gases surrounding Earth.

biofuel crops
Crops that are grown to be made into fuels.

climate change
Changes to the usual weather patterns in an area.

compost
Organic matter that has decomposed, leaving a rich source of nutrients.

cover crops
Crops grown to enrich soil and to cover it to prevent erosion.

crop rotation
Growing a different crop each season in the same area.

degraded
Run down or reduced to a lower quality.

developed countries
Countries with industrial development, a strong economy, and a high standard of living.

ecosystems
All the living and nonliving things in an area, and their connections with each other.

emissions
Substances released into the environment.

erosion
The process of rock and soil being carried away by wind and water.

feedlots
Small areas where farm animals are kept and fed grains and vegetables.

fertilizer
A substance added to soil that contains nutrients necessary for plant growth.

food security
Guarantee of food supply.

food staple
The main food eaten by people in an area.

food web
The pattern of connections between living things and their food sources.

greenhouse gases
Gases that help trap heat in Earth's atmosphere.

intensively cropped
Continuous use of land to produce food, which gradually removes nutrients from soil.

organic matter
Material from living things.

overfishing
Taking too many fish from one area or species, leading to a decrease in numbers.

rangelands
Broad areas of land used by grazing animals; can be made up of grasslands, forests, and scrublands.

salinity
The amount of salt in soil.

sewage
Human waste.

soil fertility
The amount of nutrients available in soil for plant growth.

species
Living things of the same type that can reproduce.

sustainable
Does not use more resources than Earth can regenerate.

Index

A
Africa, 7, 13, 15, 20, 21
artificial fertilizers, 12, 27, 28
Australia, 7, 9, 20

B
Benin, 15
biofuel crops, 12
Britain, 6, 25
brown streak virus, 21
bycatch, 16–19

C
Canada, 27
cassava crops, 21
cattle, 8, 9, 10
climate change, 5, 6, 7, 20–23
cover crops, 14, 15
crop diversity, 23
crop rotation, 14
crop yields, 15, 20

D
developed countries, 24
droughts, 20, 21
dryland areas, 13

E
early grazing, 9
emissions, 6, 24
erosion, 6, 9, 14
exports, 20, 25

F
farmers' markets, 26, 29
farming practices, 10, 12, 14
feedlots, 8, 11
fishery observers, 19
fish farming, 18
food miles, 24–27
food security, 11, 26
food shortages, 5
food transportation, 6, 24–27, 29

G
Global Seed Vault, 23
grain-fed animals, 8
grazing animals, 6, 7, 8–11
greenhouse gases, 4, 24, 30

I
increasing yields, 15
irrigation, 12, 13

L
land management, 13, 14
local production, 22, 26, 28

M
meat consumption, 8–11, 28
meat production, 9–11
Mediterranean Sea, 6, 17
mixed farms, 10, 22

N
natural fertilizer, 10
Norway, 23

O
Oceana, 19, 30
organic matter (in soil), 14
overfishing, 5, 6, 16–18
overgrazing, 9, 12

P
plant-based diets, 11
population growth, 5, 11, 16
preserving food, 27, 29

R
rabbits, 9
rangelands, 9–11
restoring land, 14–15

S
salinity, 13
seasonal food, 27–29
seed storage, 22, 23
sharks, 6, 16, 17, 18, 19
soil degradation, 5, 7, 12–14
soil improvement, 14–15
sub-Saharan Africa, 7, 21
sustainable fishing, 18
Sustainable Food and Agriculture Project, 22
sustainable meat production, 10

T
Tanzania, 21
targeted fishing, 18

U
United States, 12
urban agriculture, 26

V
velvet beans, 15

W
West Asia and North Africa region, 7, 13